# LOVE-EXPLAINED

BY

## MARK MORGAN

*SLOPPY BOOKS LLC*

# CONTENTS

Preface    1

Google It    5

Expectations and Prejudices    9

The Jumper Cables Analogy    15

The Job Analogy    17

Process of Elimination Not Selection    21

Why We Love    23

What Does Love Mean to You?    25

How Do You Know You are in Love?    30

Brain Chemistry    37

Psychology    38

Narcissism    40

Parents    42

Jealousy    44

What is Hate?    46

The Truths    49

Adding New Information    59

Questions    62

Closing    80

BIASC Category:  Family & Relationships / Love & Romance


Library of Congress Control Number: 2016908470
ISBN:  978-0-9974777-0-2
eBook ISBN: 978-0-9974777-1-9


Drawings by Matthew Ubertaccio


Manufactured in the United States of America


10  9  8  7  6  5  4  3  2  1

# LOVE-EXPLAINED

# Preface

In opening this book you may be asking yourself, who is this guy and what makes him an expert on love? My response is to ask you, who are the experts on love? Are you one? Are your parents, friends, pastors or teachers love experts? How about psychologists like Freud or writers like Shakespeare? And what do relationship experts like John Gray (*Men are from Mars, Women are from Venus*) or Leo Buscaglia (*Dr. Love*) say that love is exactly?

They don't say, but in this book, I will.

You would think knowing what love is exactly would draw a lot of interest from the great thinkers of our time, but there is no agreement. They are just as likely to be confused and want to be in love as the next person. When asked by their spouse, "Why do you love me?" they are just as likely to become uncomfortable and stop thinking as the next person. Well, I did not stop thinking. Anytime answers were supplied to me that did not make sense, it only made me more curious. I did not stop thinking about love because I never received an answer that could be proven. This was of primary importance to me in writing this book. I felt that any explanation of love should have to prove itself. Much like a scientific paper, I want to build a case, propose a hypothesis, and give examples to prove my hypothesis is accurate, thereby proving to you what love is.

Many people use poems or quotes to describe love. Some examples are shown below.

*"Love is composed of a single soul inhabiting two bodies"*
- Aristotle, Greek philosopher 384BC-322BC

*"A loving heart is the beginning of all knowledge"*
- Thomas Carlyle, Scottish philosopher 1795-1881

*"Love conquers all"*
- Virgil, Roman poet 70BC-19BC

These quotes are nice, but do they explain love or hold-up under all conditions? Of course not! We do not combine souls, you can have knowledge without love, and love does not conquer all.

*"Love is a many splendored thing"*
- 1955 romance film

*"Love is from the heart"*

*"Love is blind"*
- Geoffrey Chaucer, English poet 1343-1400

Again, these are lovely quotes, but they do not explain love either. How well do these common explanations for love hold up under all conditions? They don't, so I can't stop thinking there.

My hypothesis or explanation of love will hold up under all conditions. I will explain romantic love, parental love, love of pets, football teams, cars and more. Unlike a scientific paper, I will explain it in a way that is easy for all to understand.

Before we get started let's try some quotes with a different take on what love might be.

*"The best things can't be told.*
*The second best are misunderstood.*
*The third best are what we talk about."*
- Heinrich Zimmer, German indologist 1890-1943 from "an open life - Joseph Campbell in conversation with Michael Toms"

*"A kiss is a lovely trick designed by nature to stop speech when words become superfluous."*
- Ingrid Bergman, Sweedish actress 1915-1982

*"Do you know what it means to come home at night to a woman who'll give you a little love, a little affection, a little tenderness? It means you're in the wrong house, that's what it means."*
- Henny Youngman, American comedian 1906-1998

*Greetings, I'm Stan, this is my lady Irene and my dog Max. We are here to guide you through the book and add a little humor on the way.*

# GOOGLE IT

If you were to Google "What is love?" on your computer you would get a lot of theories. Most of them involving multiple kinds of love. Bear with me a few lines, I need to describe these theories and types of love to make my point.

The writer C.S. Lewis says there are four types of love: affection, friendship, erotic and love of god.

The Greeks say there are four types of love: Agape, Eros, Phila and Storge.

Psychologist Dr Carmen Herra says there are four types: transitory, karmic, compromise and soulful.

The interactive bible says there are three types: the if kind, the because of kind and the in spite of kind of love.

And in the book *Colors of Love* J. A. Lee defined six types of love: Eros, Lundus, Storge, Pragma, Mania and Agape.

All these types of love make these explanations cumbersome. Moreover, to combine them into one simple theory seems impossible. And that does not address the most obvious question of all, why do we need so many types of love? Why isn't there a theory that covers all situations and answer all questions, with one and only one explanation?

This is my inspiration for writing this book. I could not get a simple answer for the question, "What is love?" By the end of this book I will have one simple straightforward explanation for you and I will use words you have heard of to do it.

One difficulty in finding a single definition is that the concept of love is flexible. You might love your spouse, your children, your friends, yourself, your country, your sports team, your car, your pets or your garden. Some may even love violence or masochism. Your love can be romantic, faithful, passionate, friendly, a crush or in any form imaginable.

Some people do not seem to love at all and yet some fall in love at the drop of a hat. But what everyone has in common is that each one of us learns what love is on our own. There were no classes or books to teach you what love is, until this book. Your mom or dad did not sit you down and tell you what love is. As a child I asked my mom, "Is the love I feel for you the same as the love you feel for daddy?" I still remember the look she gave me, and it was left to me to find the answer.

When you are dating age, your parents might ask you if you love your boyfriend/girlfriend,  and if he/she loves you. They might steer you towards someone they think is better for you (or them). Or steer you away from someone they think is bad for you (or them). Your parents might have built up more knowledge than you on relationships, but they do not know how to measure love any more than you or I do. Note to self: Invent a love meter.

The reality is that each person creates his/her own definition of love based on what he or she has learned. An individual's criteria for love could include: security, fidelity, intimacy, commitment, sexuality, stability, compatibility, or social standing. This list could go on and on to include anything you could expect from another person.

Society says you should expect your relatives to be people who will always love you, but there is no guarantee of love from family members. The unlimited number of different family scenarios means any emotion is possible between you and a relative. You could love your mother, hate your mother, or not even know her. You could be close to your siblings, hate them, not know them at all, or could care less. You can love or hate anyone at any level. Just because you are related does not guarantee anything.

Going forward in this book, since there are many types of loving relationships, I am going to use the word **spouse** when I refer to any individuals in a romantic and/or sexual relationship. Whether it be between a man and wife, boyfriend and girlfriend, two women or two men.

Irene tries out a new invention on Stan.

Irene: *"This device says you really love me honey."*

# EXPECTATIONS & PREJUDICES

One of the ways you can understand and organize your world is through your expectations. You use expectations, such as traditions and rules, to guide you through life. They help you anticipate what you (and others) are supposed to do in a particular situation and going in to the future.

There are many examples of how you use expectations. If you are playing baseball, you expect of yourself and the other players to use the rules of the game. The hitter will run to first base after he hits the ball. A pitcher will throw from the rubber, you get three outs and the rest of the rules of the game. I am having expectations that everyone reading this book will have at least this knowledge of baseball.

You expect the sun will rise tomorrow morning and will go down tomorrow evening. If you are honest, you want others to be honest. When you drive down the road in your correct lane you expect others to drive down the road in their correct lane also. You get these expectations from your life experiences, your parents, your peers, the television and so on.

I have the expectation that if I was in a burning building, a firefighter or relative would run in and save me. And I expect of myself to run in to a burning building to save a relative. But the expectations for a stranger to save me or for me to save the stranger are less than the expectations I have for my relatives. I expect more from my loving relatives than I do from strangers. And I know others share my view.

What if you left the lights on in your car all day and you needed the battery jumped in order to start your car. You would expect a friend or relative to help you much more than you would expect a stranger to help you. And what if your expectation of the stranger is one of a bad experience? What if you were afraid to ask the stranger for the cables because you feared for your safety? What if you are afraid of someone because of his/her age, tattoos, color of his/her skin or style of clothing? Your expectation for the stranger has produced a negative stereotype or prejudice.

A prejudice by itself is not bad, it is just judging something ahead of time (pre-judge). Despite the fact that our politically correct society disdains this kind of thinking, a prejudice often benefits us or can save our lives. If you were to ask the wrong person for jumper cables, you could be taken advantage of, mugged, raped or killed.

A prejudice could keep you alive if you were thinking about walking in to a lion's cage. Just the thought (the expec-tation) of what could happen in there will influence your behavior. After all, the lion could maul and kill you. You have prejudged the lion as a killer. Think of the evolutionary advantage to having this prejudice. The person who is afraid of the lion might survive while the unafraid person might lose his/her life going in the lion's cage. The fearful person passes his/her genes and wisdom on to the next generation while the fearless person might not. Prejudice/expectations against lions, playing in traffic, strangers, falling from high places, eating bad food, going in to dangerous situations or lightning save our children and our lives every day.

While society says prejudices are bad, I say that is just the way we are. As you go through life, you learn about people and situations. Your experiences give you information on a person, that they are friendly, mean, loving, happy, smart, dumb or boring. As you get to know this person more, you can either add new information to your growing perception of them, or you can stop thinking of them as an individual and stereotype them. It's a lot easier to stereotype in most situations because you do not have time to get to know every person. But once you stereotype, it takes a lot of effort to change your mind, to search out and add new information about a person or circumstance. So you don't do it, unless you have to. You normally put the person in a category and you stop adding information to it.

If you have stereotyped a person as friendly, you tend to look for friendly characteristics in order to feel good about your self-knowledge and belief system. If you see non friendly behavior that is contrary to your beliefs in the person, you develop cognitive dissonance and create a relieving statement such as "He's normally not like this" or "He's having a bad day." That way you can feel good about yourself, keep your belief system intact, and relieve the dissonance you feel from receiving contrary information. In this case it's more important to preserve your ego than it is to add factual information to it.

I believe when you are in romantic love, you are using a part of the same prejudiced learning system you naturally use already. In this case you see the good side of the person, and you overlook the bad. You learn to love the same way you learn about everything else. You get an opinion, you get expectations from it, then you defend it.

To further illustrate how you naturally get opinions and defend them, how many lifelong Republicans or Democrats do you know who are switching parties? How many people practice a different religion than their parents? Or, how many people cheer for a different sports team than they cheered for as a kid? Very few.

*"We naturally like what we have been accustomed to, and attracted towards it. [...] The same is the case with those opinions of man to which he has been accustomed from his youth; he likes them, defends them, and shuns the opposite views."*
- Maimonides, The Guide to the Perplexed, Jewish philosopher 1135-1204

Before you move on, I wish to further illustrate how natural expectations are to how everyone lives their lives. We humans are curious creatures with a need to explain everything that happens to us and to anticipate our future. As we go through life we gain knowledge and we use it to help guide us in our future decisions. This knowledge becomes our expectations for the world. It helps us to anticipate what is going to happen next, how I am supposed to act, how others are supposed to act, what I am supposed to wear, when and where I am to go. The following is a partial list of words that describe expectations for ourselves, others and society. Where would you be without your customs, rules, fears, traditions, ceremonies, principles, standards, unwritten rules, laws, loyalty, routines, rituals, mores, honesty, guidelines, models, values, practices, paranoia and policies? "Like a feather blowing in the wind." The point here is, love, like an expectation from the list above, is a natural memory tool you use to help guide you through life.

Stan: *"Hey look Irene, It's Tony the tiger."*

# THE JUMPER CABLES ANALOGY

Let's say you have left your car lights on some-where and return to the car to find the battery is dead and your car will not start. You do not have jumper cables so you proceed to ask a stranger in the parking lot if they have any. The stranger says no, but as they leave you are able to see somehow that the stranger did have the cables. You are likely to be upset that the stranger did not help you out. Your emotions could vary widely: anger, disappointment or sadness, depending on the expectations you have of that stranger.

Now instead imagine the same scenario except you asked your mother for the jumper cables. She says no and leaves but somehow you know she did have the jumper cables. You would likely be devastated. How could she do this? How could she leave me here? You have such high expectations of her, that for her to lie to you and not be there for you, would shatter your illusions of her and make you question her love for you. So, as it turns out, the higher the expectations you have for a person, the more disappointed you would be by their lying. If it is a stranger you might not care at all. "That stranger was just a creep anyway," you might say to yourself. But to say that about your mother would be going down a path away from love.

So it seems the more you love something, the higher the expectations you have for it. For example, you have many expectations for a spouse or parent. They are supposed to be there for me. They are going to be there when I get home. They care about what happens to me. They are not going to hurt me. They will take care of me if were sick, for example.

To help make my point, let's go at expectations from the opposite direction. How about if you had a spouse or parent that did not care what happened to you or that would leave you behind in the parking lot without jumper cables? What if you did not know if your spouse or parent would come home tonight? What if your spouse, parent or sibling did not care if you were injured? Would you think this person loved you? No.

Another example of expectations in the opposite direction is when you have no expectations for yourself in a relationship. What if you would not be there for friends or loved ones if they needed you? What if you do not care if they are hurt or if you hurt their feelings? What if you acted this way? Does this sound like someone you are in love with? No. And would someone treated this way feel you are loving them? No.

# THE JOB ANALOGY

Let's say our cartoon friend Stan is applying for a job.

He says to himself, "Well, if I get this job, I'll be able to quit working two jobs. Then I can spend more time with my family, maybe even coach a sports team. Irene and I could move in to a nice house in a nice neighborhood. The kids could play in the front yard. Have barbeques on the back patio. This job also has paid vacations, and I might be able to take a decent two week vacation when I earn it, and see my mom back home. It's been too long since I've seen her. This job's gonna be great, I feel great." (Please feel free to go back to the top of the paragraph and replace with dreams relevant to you.)

But then he didn't get the job.

What happened? Stan had all these expectations for this job. It was going to change his and his family's lives for the better.

What happened? According to my theory, Stan fell in love with the new job. He projected expectations about how this job is going to help him, help his family, and make him feel better about himself. And the job even made him happy while he was thinking about it.

Notice in the initial expectations there are no negatives about the job. No, "I'll have to commute thirty-five minutes each day," "I'll have to bite my tongue with my supervisors" or "I can't eat breakfast with Irene during the week anymore." Instead the negatives are minimized by saying to our self, "I'll use that commute to catch up on my reading" or "I can eat breakfast with Irene on the weekend."

Instead of looking through the rose colored glasses you can be best prepared for situations like job hunting by having a realistic view of your world based on facts. Author/ Psychiatrist M Scott Peck would call this "having an accurate map." By having a truthful, realistic view of what is going on in your world you can make your decisions based on the most facts.

But unfortunately those in need of a job or good news the most are the ones who use the rose colored glasses the most. After all, if you are down on your luck, in need of love or on hard times you need to imagine a better future. Anybody have any lottery tickets?

Now instead of a job analogy, Irene tells a story of Frank, a boy she met before Stan.

While they were dating, Irene would say to herself, "If I marry Frank, I will not have to feel alone anymore, I'll have a sexual partner, I'll have a good father for my children, someone to help me have and keep up a home, someone to help me feel good about myself and nurture my goals, someone I'm proud to be with, someone who makes me laugh, someone to take vacations with. This is gonna be great. I feel great." (Please feel free to go back to the top of the paragraph and replace this with any of your personal dreams here.)

But Frank didn't work out.

What happened? Irene had all these expectations for Frank. He was going to change her life for the better. He made her feel better about herself and her family.

What happened? According to my theory Irene fell in love with Frank. Irene projected expectations for Frank, about how he was going to help her, help her family, and help her feel better about herself. And he even made her feel better while she thought about a future with him.

Notice there are few negatives spoken about Frank in the beginning of the relationship. No, "Frank always leaves the toilet seat up," "He cusses a lot" or "I don't really like Frank's family that much." In initial love the negatives are minimized. Instead Irene was thinking, "I'll just put the seat down for him," "I'll get used to his bad language" or "I'll learn to love his family."

To best increase the success of a long term relationship, it is best to have the most realistic view as possible of your spouse now. The more realistic map you have of him/her now the better prepared you are, the less surprises you'll have in the future and the less likely the future will reveal something that is a deal breaker. Unfortunately, those in need of love the most are the ones who project unrealistic expectations the most.

These analogies on dating and getting a job show how it can be difficult when you are searching for a potential job or companion. You can have expectations for them but you only have so much power over the outcome. After all, a job or potential spouse has expectations too, and you might not be in them.

The analogies used prior suggest that when we have realistic and unrealistic expectations for someone, we are feeling love. But I would say that creating expectations to guide us through our life, whether realistic or unrealistic, is the way we organize our world all the time. It's just that when we are having expectations for a potential spouse we label our behavior as love.

*"Expectations are the root of all heartache."*
- paraphrase of William Shakespeare, English writer 1564-1616

# PROCESS OF ELIMINATION NOT SELECTION

Our society says you should love your parents, your children, your country, your grandparents, your God, your siblings and your spouse. You might love your neighbors, your pets, your garden or your sports team. But, by any standard of decency, you should only be having sex with one or maybe two of these.

Potentially, almost every person in the world could be your spouse. Most are too far away. Some are too old or too young. Some are the wrong sex (for you). Some are too ugly, related to you, too poor, married already, smoke cigarettes or whatever it takes for you to take them out of the running. And then out of that smaller group, there are still many candidates you could potentially choose from. That is if you live around people. Out of that smaller group you try to find one that also likes you. If none of your candidates chooses you, you are still out of luck. You need to find a new group somewhere; try a new bar, move to a new town, try a dating service or go on-line.

I believe there are many people you meet during your life that you imagine as potential spouses. You see them and think, "I could fall in love with that person under the right circumstances." Many times you do not seriously consider this person as available because they are married, you are married, they are celebrities, they are too old or too young. So society or our morals tell you not to pursue these potential mates. But sometimes people pursue these mates anyway, even when society tells them not to. I know I could fall in love with celebrity/actress Jennifer Aniston. Hey, Jennifer, give me a call.

# WHY WE LOVE

We humans are social beings so very few of us wish to live alone, or live our life without a spouse. We evolved to be social and in social groups, which is a likely reason our Homo sapien ancestors survived the other human species. Some make the case that love was needed for our species to survive but long before humans had any language, we had sex and we cared for our children. So before language there is no way the word love was needed for humans to survive as a species, maybe the actions but not the word. Animals and even plants have sex to procreate and share genetic material but no one says they are in love. Most of the time we do not give animals credit for thinking much at all. Oh, that's right, we're animals too.

But we humans do not like to think we are just like the other animals. We feel we are above this, with consciousness and intelligence unrivaled by other animals. We feel we can control our choices and determine our destinies much more than other animals so we cannot admit some animal instinct is in charge of our spousal choices. We need to feel we are in control. And we need to label it in a way that hides our instincts and selfishness and shows us in a better light.

Why we love comes down to whether we want to say it is caused by nature and/or nurture. Nature has certainly designed us to mate like any animal and to herd like many animals. But our nurture has taught us to call this process love.

Stan nods off so Donatello the turtle makes his move.

# WHAT DOES LOVE MEAN TO YOU?

*What is love to you?*
*What do you need to fall in love?*
*Why are we supposed to love?*
*Is love when I feel good all over?*

Don't you think everyone going into a romantic relationship would be better off if they were to fill out a questionnaire first? What would you ask? What do you want?

The loving spouse I am looking for needs to be:
1) good looking
2) faithful
3) funny
4) sexy
5) a sex partner
6) able to fill out a questionnaire
7) a person to be intimate with
8) a person to spend the rest of my life with
9) able to make me happy
10) financially stable
11) in love with me

I'm sure you have a few criteria of your own to add to the list.

And what might be our society's lofty expectations for you? You and your spouse need to:

1) be married

2) be faithful to each other

3) be old enough but not too old

4) have a heterosexual spouse

5) have just one spouse

6) have kids

7) spend the rest of your life with them

8) be same religion

9) be the same race or color

and more that you can add.

We also have expectations of love for our parents. I expect my parents to:

1) love me forever

2) stay with my other parent the rest of their lives

3) love all the children equally

4) be faithful to their spouse

5) provide for me (be the wallet carrier)

6) make me happy

and whatever else you think your parent should do for you.

The primary thing to notice about the expectations in the lists above is that not all of these expectations are realistic or allow for others. That is because they do not have to be. They are individual to you. Your expectations for your spouse, your relationships, and other people, are whatever you have been taught or dreamed of. Expectations do not have to be realistic.

Where do you get these expectations from? Everywhere. Your parents, your grandparents, your friends, the television, your religion and so on. A boy might grow up looking at what his mother did for him as an expectation for what he wants or does not want in his spouse. A boy might look at his father's behavior as an example of how he thinks he should or should not love his spouse. A girl might look at her mother as an example of how she wants to act in a relationship, or her mother might be the opposite of how she wants to act. Or, a girl might look at her father as an example of what she wants or does not want in a spouse. We all grow up in our own unique family environments and each of us creates our own ideal expectations for our family, love and relationships based on those unique experiences.

This also reveals a primary reason it is so difficult to give love a consistent definition. How can you have a unified definition if each person has his/her own definition?

*"There are all kinds of love in this world but never the same love twice."*
- F. Scott Fitzgerald, American writer (1896-1940) The Great Gatsby

Love is hard to define, if you bother to define it at all. Some people do not even want to define love, feeling you cannot have love unless it is a mystery. Some people are waiting for cupid's arrow to hit them or for butterflies in their stomach. Some feel love is supposed to know what to do all by itself, and others feel love will jointly take them and their partner over when the appropriate time comes.

But there can be a point to avoid discussing love. Have you ever asked your spouse why they love you? Why they are really there? The more detail you get, the more you pry, it seems the farther away from love you get. Do you really want to know all the selfish reasons they are in this relationship with you? No, just the good ones. Do you really want to tell all the reasons why you need to be in this relationship? No, just the good ones. These conversations rarely make any relationship more intimate, and we learn to avoid them because it is mutually beneficial.

Irene: *"I can't tell you what I want, cause then you'll know. How will I know if you're doing something because I told you or because you love me?"*

# How Do You Know You Are In Love?

*What happens to make you think you are in love?*
*Why do you think you are in love?*
*How do you know your spouse loves you?*

*Is it when someone makes you feel good?*
*Is it when you have butterflies in your stomach?*

Do I know someone loves me when they tell me that they love me? How do they know? How do I know they are telling the truth? What if I tell them I love them? Does that mean I love them? How do I know?

What if only one person says I love you? Is the couple in love now? What if one person says I love you, and the other person does not respond with an I love you back? Now that has got to be one of life's most awkward moments. Having only one spouse profess his/her love puts a lot of pressure on the other spouse to show his/her intentions. Will they ever love me? This is a situation that has pressure on it to rectify itself. Either we get both spouses to say I love you or the relationship might end soon.

Irene: *"Our love makes everything better."*
Stan: *"Our love can conquer anything."*
Landlord: *"How about your love conquering this month's rent over here."*

One of the things that informs you that you are in love is when you (or your spouse) change behavior. If our cartoon character Stan normally goes to poker every Friday night but now he wants to be with Irene instead, he and Irene notice his changing. If Stan goes out of his way to make Irene happy or think of her when he normally would not put out such effort, he and Irene notice his change. If Stan is nicer, more available, cleaner, stops smoking and stops looking at other women, he and Irene notice his change. And when Stan and Irene broke up for awhile, but eventually got back together, they noticed how this relationship is different than previous relationships. Also, when the guys start telling Stan that he is whipped because he is spending all his time with Irene, it is just the guys noticing his changes.

To help prove how important change is, let us go at this from the opposite direction. Let's say Stan did not want to change for Irene. Irene wants Stan to change his poker night but he will not do it. She wants Stan to be nicer, cleaner, more available and stop going out with other women but he will not change. Is this the way you would expect Stan to act if he is in love? No.

*"When we love someone our love becomes demonstrable or real only through our exertion – through the fact that for that someone (or for our self) we take an extra step or walk an extra mile. Love is not effortless. To be contrary, love is effort-full."*

- M Scott Peck, psychologist (1936-2005) - The Road Less

Traveled: A new psychology of love, traditional values and spiritual growth, 1978

Leon Festinger in his cognitive dissonance theory would say, "You come to love what you suffer for." His theory states that when you spend time with people or things, you are investing in them, and by that you can grow to love them. The more time you invest in this person or thing, the more time there is to grow the love. Time spent weeding your garden, working on your car, working for a charity, being part of a club or cheering for your team shows you are invested and that you care. Emotions are there as your club, garden, or team, succeeds or fails, wins or loses. Endocrinologist studies state that some sports fans are so emotionally invested while watching the game, their hormone responses are the same as the players competing in the game. This theory shows how, by investing time, you can grow to love people and things other than people. Any Chicago Cub fans out there relating to the suffer for part of this theory?

While you are suffering for your cause you are often involved with other people in the same cause. Camaraderie is built as you share your time and emotions with them. Benefits shared can include personal pride, identifying with others, belonging to a group, regional pride and mutual dislike of others. That is why you enjoy it when you are around people who share your enthusiasm for your: political party, god, sports team, school club or Labrador retrievers. They make you feel good because they confirm your beliefs

33

and love the same thing you do.

## *Absence makes the heart grow fonder...*

is the old saying. And I could not agree more. When you are used to having someone around, and now they are gone, it can reveal feelings about them you did not know you had.

I am sure you have had at least one instance where a friend or family member has moved away or died, or a spouse has broken up with you. The comfort and companionship you experienced with this person is now gone, leaving a void in your life, remembering the times you had with them. But when you remember them without them being there, your thoughts can become unrealistic. You might remember all the nice things they did for you or the way you felt at ease with them, totally forgetting any of their character flaws.

This is a great example of when your love is growing, when you are believing all the good expectations you have for someone and disbelieving all the bad expectations you have for them.

And love can grow really fast when you are missing your spouse. If you moved away or you initiated a break up with your spouse, you might be prepared to fill the void since you were somewhat anticipating it. But if someone else makes that decision for you, if someone else asked for the breakup, then the void produced can be temporarily devastating. If you were hurt by this person leaving, soon might come a time where your thoughts turn from the unrealistic good to the unrealistic bad, remembering only the bad times and none of the good.

Remembering the bad can help sometimes because it preserves your ego. If you were to feel you needed this person long after they have moved on from you it is unhealthy and damaging to your ego. By creating expectations for the person that are bad and having none that are good diminishes them and preserves your ego. If you asked Irene about her ex-boyfriend Frank now she would say "That guy cussed way too much for me" and "I would have never been able to get along with his family."

Think of how much tougher it would be on you if your spouse died in the midst of your relationship rather than after a breakup. Sorry about the morbid thoughts. But if his/her death happened after a breakup, you might have resolved your expectations for him/her knowing that you did not have a future with them. But if a successful relationship has ended suddenly, the loss could scar forever. Think of how we feel about the deaths of John F Kennedy, Abraham Lincoln, Jim Morrison, Martin Luther King, Amelia Earhart, James Dean, or any child. We had so much more planned for them. We had such expectations. Their legends are larger than many who lived long lives.

*"He who lives in our mind is near though he may actually be far away; but he who is not in our heart is far though he may really be nearby."*
- Chanakya, Indian philosopher (370BC – 283BC)

# BRAIN CHEMISTRY

Let's change direction away from expectations and people dying to discuss how some modern scientists study emotions like love. Sorry romanticists, scientists are not looking at the heart for emotions like love. Maybe the stomach, but not the heart. Science has proven that our thoughts about love, hate or anything are located in the brain. And that our thoughts are both chemical and electrical. But as my old chemistry teacher used to say, "Everything is chemical or physical."

In researching the brain, scientists have made many great discoveries, but they have not found the love spot. The brain is such a complicated organ it makes for a very tough task. They can send electricity to spots in your brain or give you drugs to make you feel good but that does not identify something as complicated as love.

As you can tell, what I know about brain chemistry, you could put in a thimble and have room left over for an elephant. But that is fine. I just wanted to show that scientists who study emotions are studying it in the brain and not the heart. This should not be big news. I will leave it to the scientists to research love using electricity and chemistry. I will use common situations that we all know well.

# PSYCHOLOGY

Again in this chapter I am not going to claim any knowledge of Sigmund Freud's analysis of the human mind. Oedipus is a great theory, but I do not know anybody who ever said it influenced them. I do not know any boy who secretly wanted to have sex with his mom or any girl who wanted to have sex with her dad. Maybe it is out there, maybe it is subconscious, but I have not seen it so it is not going into my theory.

Some people need love and companionship more than others. Most people are not happy being alone for long periods of time, and, moreover, solitary confinement is a torture. But everybody is different in how much they need to be around people, accepted in the crowd or paired up with a spouse. I knew some individuals who could not break up an ongoing relationship until they had started their next relationship. They could not be alone. People who do not feel comfortable alone are more likely to put themselves out in the crowd, around new people or on a dating service than a person who is comfortable alone. That way they can find new friends or search for a spouse.

# NARCISISSM

The most important driver of all your actions, including how you love, is your narcissism, or ego (thanks, Freud). We are taught that only a few of us act in this extremely selfish way, but all of us have an ego to preserve. After all, the most important thing in the world to you is your self, how you feel, how you perceive yourself, how you look, are you safe, is your stuff safe, how things linked to you are thought of, and so on. This is who you are. What else are you, if not the accumulation of what you think of yourself and what others think of you?

And if your self is everything to you, then you need to defend it and preserve it if you are to appear good to yourself and others. If you don't, who else will? You do this by trying to make yourself look good and by making things you are associated with look good. You do this by defending your opinion and creating biases to defend your opinion. By elevating yourself or cutting others down so you can feel superior. If you think of yourself as reputable and if others think of you as reputable, you feel good about yourself. Therefore, if your parents, your spouse, your kids, your friends, your favorite football team or your garden are praiseworthy, your narcissism says you feel good about yourself because they are a part of you, and you have invested in them.

But selfishness is not a quality that endears you to others, so when you are selfish, you want to hide it. Sometimes you can be selfish even when you are doing things for others or giving. Either you want others to think well of you, or you think it gets you into heaven.

You do not go in to a romantic relationship selfishly saying, *I'm only here for myself.* You cannot say, *I'm only here because I want sex,* it makes you look like an animal. You cannot say, *I feel uncomfortable alone, I need someone to be with me.* You sound like you have mental problems. You cannot say, *I need you to support me because I don't want to work,* you look lazy. These words do not preserve a proper image of yourself, of others or of a healthy relationship. You must look as if you have good intentions instead of selfish ones. You need a way to cover up this mutual selfishness so both sides look good to themselves and to society. How about we call it love?

One could make the case that the reduction of narcissism is not only important in growing up, but also is a key component to love. When you reduce thoughts of yourself and think of others, you show them you care, you show you are loving them, no matter who or what they are.

*"Whoever loves becomes humble. Those who love have, so to speak, pawned a part of their narcissism."*
- Sigmund Freud, father of psychoanalysis (1856-1939)

# Parents

Parents are often narcissistic/self loving in raising their children and grandchildren, and some of their love for them can be explained this way. The child was helpless when born so it needed the parent to survive. The parent has invested lots of time with the child and has high expectations for it. Almost every parent wants the best for their child and if the child succeeds then it will reflect back on the parents as their success also. They ideally want their child to be the star of the ballgame, be smart, be a doctor and marry the best looking of the opposite sex. It makes the parent look good.

Sometimes kids do not live up to these expectations and become normal instead of exceptional. If so, then the parents need to grow up a little and lose some of the narcissism in order to have a healthy relationship with their children.

Children, on the other hand, have different expectations for their parents than a parent has for his/her child. That is because the parent has invested a lot of time in the child, while the child has invested nothing. Parents have expectations for their child because of the potential future of his/her child and what he/she might accomplish. While a child's expectations, and love, for his/her parent are based on what the parent is doing for his/her currently or have done for them already.

It's hard to raise good parents nowadays.

There are also the expectations the parent has of his/her self that let the parent know they love the child. After all, a parent would run in to a burning building for his/her child, but they might not for a stranger's child. I personally would have what I called "mothering dreams" when my son was an infant. That means I would dream and imagine every circumstance where my son was in danger and I had to rescue him. I knew it was up to me and no one else to rescue my child. Higher expectations on me, the parent, let me know my relationship with my child is different and stronger than it is for other children.

A parent can also recognize the love for a child by a change in his/her own behavior. If a parent goes out of the way to be with a child when they would normally be elsewhere, they are showing the child love. But many times a parent has to go into the workforce to bring in money for the family. So the working parent might have to show his/her love for the family by working longer instead of being home. After all, that is what they feel they need to do to achieve what is best for the family. But when a parent spends a lot of time away from the family working, this behavior can be thought of as abandonment, depending on how it is handled. Whether you recognize long hours of work away from the family as love or abandonment goes back to what your expectations are for yourself, your spouse, and your family.

# JEALOUSY

Talking about narcissism and selfishness leads to an explanation for jealousy. That is because jealousy is where narcissism meets love. After all, if you are defending yourself and your stuff, you are not going to want someone around who could take your beloved spouse away. And your spouse does not want someone around who could take you away. You have invested in each other. Sometimes jealousy is intentionally orchestrated, and sometimes it is accidental, but either way, the thought of your spouse leaving you for another person is a great loss of self esteem.

Often times jealousy or a break up can bring up emotions for your spouse you did not know you had before. The emotions of jealousy or abandonment are often the first symptoms you notice that you might be in love. During a relationship you might have taken a spouse for granted, but if they are away, if you break up or if they are with another person, you miss them more than you thought you would. Everybody reacts differently to jealousy and abandonment because we are all individuals, but the emotions they create in us can make us feel we might be in love.

To help prove the point about jealousy and love, let's go at it from the opposite direction. What happens if you are not jealous if your spouse is dating another person. Or, your spouse is not jealous of you dating another person. Does this sound like a loving relationship? No. Most societies say it is normal for spousal relationships to be monogamous, so if your spouse is around someone who could violate that monogamy it is normal to be jealous. A relationship with more than one sex partner could function if that is what you both want, but its not what we are taught to imagine as love.

Jealousy does not always have to be towards your lover. You can be jealous of anything someone else has that you wish you had. You can be jealous of someone's car, house, money or whatever you value. You can be jealous of a sports team or its fans if they are winning and you are not. It has been interesting in recent years watching basketball fans be jealous of basketball star Le Bron James as he decided which team to play for. Fans loyal (loving) to a team wanted him to play for their basketball team and nowhere else. When he did choose a team to play for everyone lined up to cheer against him, except for the fans of the team he is playing on now.

*"Those people hate us more than they like themselves."*
- Mack Brown, former University of Texas football coach, talking on the radio about his rivals

Your narcissism can also make you jealous of others success, because for others to succeed it means you might be perceived as failing. Heck, this might even stop some people I know from buying this book. They don't want to know a successful writer, they want to be one themselves.

# WHAT IS HATE?

Seems to me if you claim to have a definition for love, then you should also have a definition for hate. In a previous chapter, I made a case that the absence of someone you like can let you know you love them. So therefore I contend that being around something you do not like too much can make you hate it. If you do not like someone or something but you can get away from them you will not build up hate. Two people who dislike each other but never see each other or have to deal with each other will not build up the tension needed to create hate. Two countries that are far apart rarely go to war but those who have to live next to each other like Israel and Palestine have developed hatred towards each other. They cannot get away from each other.

When I was a kid, we visited my sister's house for Christmas. She gave her son (my nephew) a turntable and two 45-rpm records as presents. One of the records was a top song of the day I liked called "Green Eyed Lady" by Sugar-loaf. My nephew proceeded to play that song over and over again that Christmas day until I hated it. I could not get away from it. The more I would hear that song, the more it would bother me until, *If I hear that song again, I'll go crazy*. If you want a soundtrack for this book, put "Green Eyed Lady" on and play it over and over again while you read the book.

Proximity is also why spousal relationships can grow hate faster than other relationships. You cannot get away from your spouse. You come in to relationships with expectations for what your relationships will be, but many times you or your spouse do not live up to these expectations. In the beginning you overlook the little things, but after awhile, you have to reestablish your boundaries. By not being able to get away from your spouse, the little things can grow big until they become frustrating to you. When this frustration is unending it can grow hate or depression instead of love.

Hey guys, don't forget to put the seat down.

Hate can also grow in other things we can not get away from. We often cannot get away from parents, siblings, cars, co workers, fans of another team, relatives or neighbors. And these are certainly people (things) capable of frustrating us or depressing us. So if you are stuck with someone (something) you do not want to be with, be careful you are not growing hate instead of love.

Hate can also be produced when you are frustrated by your expectations not being met. If you grow up with a set of values such as fairness, patriotism, honesty, religious affiliation or hard work, you can be upset when others do not have the same values or act the same as you do. Let's say you're driving your car one day and you notice another driver is not obeying the traffic rules, weaving in and out of traffic or endangering others. Does that upset you? How about if you're watching your favorite team play and it seems the referees are making every call against your team. How does that make you feel? If you have expectations of fairness and you are not being treated fairly, it can be very frustrating.

I was talking to a friend of mine one day and asked him how his weekend was. He said he had gotten into a fight and I asked what happened. He said he was at an event and the Star Spangled Banner was being played. My friend and others took off their hats for the song but one man in front of him did not take his hat off. My friend asked him (ask might be generous) to take his hat off, but he told my friend to mind his own business. The next thing you know, it had escalated into a fist fight. I asked my friend why the stranger leaving his hat on made him mad so quickly, he said his dad had made it important that my friend take his hat off for the song while he was growing up. So as it turns out, my friend had expectations for the crowd to take their hats off too. And when the other guy didn't do what my friend felt he had to do, it frustrated him. Next thing you know, his unrealistic expectations for the crowd, and some alcohol I assume, had him in a fight.

This appears to be one of the greatest problems in the world today. Not the alcohol. It is the inability of people to tolerate those different than themselves.

# THE TRUTHS

Throughout this book, I've made my case for explaining love by introducing ideas and situations to help describe my theory. I am sure you agree with some of these ideas and others you might not agree with at all. But among these ideas about love, I feel there are some truths we should be able to agree on. And with these truths, I will put together my theory for what love is exactly.

These are the truths I have accumulated from the previous chapters. Hopefully you agree with me about the following statements.

1) Scientists do not study emotions at your heart.

2) There are no love meters.

3) Love is never defined by the experts. Love is used to answer the questions.

4) Every couple, every relationship has things in common and are yet unique.

5) Each person has to learn what love is on his/her own.

6) You love all by yourself.

7) You are capable of loving anything. Any person, place or thing.

8) Expectations and prejudices are natural memory tools used to guide you through life.

9) Your expectations for your love can be realistic or unrealistic.

So if these are the facts about love, what definition or hypothesis for love can meet the criteria for all the above conditions?

What is love if it cannot be measured?

What is love if each person has to learn what love is on his/her own?

What is love if it is unique to each of us?

What is love if it is unique to each couple?

What is love if it can start and stop?

What is love if it is created like an expectation or prejudice?

What is love if the greater the expectations you have, the greater the love?

What is love if you are capable of loving anything?

What is love if you can do it all by yourself? And,

What is love if it can be realistic or unrealistic?

What is it love could possibly be to be able to answer all the above questions?

**The answer is:** Any feelings of love you have for something are being created in your own brain. It is your own expectations and emotions, whether they are realistic, unrealistic, or a combination. It is not something that is in the air or is shared. The word love is created to explain these expectations, emotions and changes in our actions in a way that makes us look good to ourselves and others.

I know this is not the romance you have been taught to believe. But any love emotion you feel can be explained in the paragraph above. I challenge you to think of your own feelings and relationships to find any evidence of love you have experienced that is not explained above.

If your spouse has expectations for you in his/her head, also, that is awesome, but you do not have feelings together. You do not think the thoughts, feel the pain or feel the feelings of your spouse. You can only think your own thoughts and feel your own feelings. You can certainly relate to, understand, and empathize with another person. You could share with your spouse the emotions you feel. Or you could know something about them that they do not admit to themselves, but you cannot feel his/her feelings.

Just because I say love is your own thoughts does not mean the relationship you are in now is any different. It is just that now you have been notified your relationship is not being held together by some mysterious force. Your relationships are what you make them. It is up to you and your spouse to make it work, you and your parent to make it work, you and your child to make it work, or you and your friend to make it work. But if you are in a successful long term relationship with anyone now, you probably know that already.

And just because love is your own thoughts does not mean you have not felt emotions, feelings, sensations, or intimacy in your relationship. You could feel joy or loneliness, jealousy or happiness. It is just that any feelings you have for this person (or thing), you are the one who created it. You could have emotions and intimacy with your friend, spouse, or pet. And you could feel like you love your friend, spouse or pet. But if you feel there is a mysterious force holding you to any one of them, it is your illusion.

*"We have our emotions, not because they are caused in us. But because they are a way of dealing with the world so that we could come to see ourselves as better than we would otherwise."*
- Jean-Paul Sarte, French philosopher (1905-1980)

Now let's go back over the truths to see if they confirm the hypothesis.

1) Scientists do not study emotions at your heart.

Thoughts come from your brain, not from your heart. You are taught that love is from the heart instead of the brain, because you never describe love as being intelligent, cognitive or rational. This is the way you deal with things logically. Love is not thought of as logical, it is often described as a mystery. Therefore, when you want to know where love resides, it cannot be from our brain. So you need to find another part of the body where it could be from.

The brain has no nerves to feel sensations, you do not even need anesthesia to operate on it, so you are never going to feel anything there. But when you get nervous, anxious or feel love, you sometimes get the sensation of butterflies in your stomach or your heart beats faster.

So therefore you are more likely to interpret your emotions as coming from your heart area than your brain, because your heart beat and the butterflies are there. Over time society has adopted the heart to describe love and many things that are not solved by logic. For example, a hard working athlete or soulful singer is said to have heart.

2) There are no love meters.

Have you ever seen or heard of a love meter? Except in a cartoon. Of course not. Scientists who study the brain wish they could measure love. But the brain is very complicated with redundant systems built in that make it difficult to pin many things down to one spot. If you want a love meter go find a scientist to make you one.

3) Love is never defined by the experts. Love is used to answer the questions.

It is hard to define something that is unique to each individual. Most people who do try have explained love with songs, poems, sonnets or romance novels. There are some who have a theory for love but their theory divides love up in to many types. As I said in the beginning of this book, I know of no one to explain love in one simple theory, before this book.

Love is a word created to answer questions for behavior we cannot explain, will not admit to or do not want to explain. When you are acting different, having expectations for something or missing someone who is not there anymore, what do you call this? You call it love. And when you are trying to convince someone about love, or convince anyone of anything, a common technique is the use of thought-terminating clichés. You can get someone to stop thinking and go along with you with cliches like: The shopper is always right, Think outside the box, That's just the way it is, I love you or I don't love you. These expressions are not debatable, they are thought-terminating. So when you use the word love to say he/she loves to go dancing, loves the new car, loves Francis, loves to run, loves to go shopping, or loves to eat, these statements are not debatable, they are the answer for the behavior.

4) Every couple, every relationship has things in common and are yet unique.

Every person has things in common with other people and yet has learned his/her own unique expectations for what he/she feel a loving relationship should be to them. Then you put person number one's unique expectations with a second person's unique expectations when you create a relationship. This creates an unlimited number of relationship combinations and expectations that are unique to each couple. This dilemma of unlimited possibilities presented a problem that was paramount to solve in writing this book. How can you have one theory that will be an explanation for everyone? I feel my theory does that.

5) Each person has to learn what love is on his/her own.

Mom and dad do not sit you down and explain how your mind is operating while you are in love and neither does anyone else. Almost everything about love that society presents to you is done with poems, songs, romance novels, greeting cards or fairy tales. With many of these stories designed to create rituals that sell you something like Valentine's cards or engagement diamonds. Until this book, you have been on your own to learn about love.

6) You love all by yourself.

You create your thoughts, expectations and emotions all by yourself. You cannot feel what another person is feeling or see things from another persons perspective. Our society, the conditions you are in, and other people influence you, but only as much as you let them. You can let a situation make you mad or you can turn it around and not let it bother you at all. You can fall in love with someone or not care at all. It is up to you if you can control it.

You have the ability to see any situation from your own unique perspective. If you are a person who perceives yourself and those around you as loving, that is great. If you perceive yourself and others around you as not loving, that is the way it is.

*"The greatest discovery of my generation is that a human being can alter his life by altering his attitudes."*
- William James, father of American psychology (1842-1910)

7) You are capable of loving anything. Any person, place or thing.

You could love your spouse, kids, butter pecan ice cream, a football team, your pet or the beach. Why not? Anything you invest in, have expectations for, or makes you feel good is a possibility. If you want to love more than one spouse or cheer for more than one football team, so be it. What ever your mind says you love, you love. Mine says butter pecan ice cream.

8) Expectations and prejudices are natural memory tools used to guide you through life.

A prejudice is not a bad thing. It is an expectation that is a necessary memory tool for having information ahead of time for anything. You need to have expectations so you can anticipate events and be prepared for them. You need to know what time to be at work, what to wear at work and how to act around your workplace. You need to know when Christmas is, how to be prepared, what to bring, the words of a Christmas song or what to wear. You need to be prepared in order to deal with people and events properly. Having expectations are how you do that.

9) Your expectations for your love can be realistic or unrealistic.

What do you imagine your spouse should be to you? Do you think your spouse should be able to make you happy, keep you company, never bore you, help you raise the kids, provide for you, be a sex partner, be an intellectual conversationalist, love you forever, always be there for you and be nice all the time? Of course not, that would be unrealistic. But it does not stop you from wanting it.

Stan: *"We don't open presents on Christmas eve, We wait till Christmas morning."*

# ADDING NEW INFORMATION

I would like to think that I have presented adequate information in the above chapters to teach you a new perspective on love. To take you away from the idea that love is from Cupid's arrow and make it understandable and realistic. But I understand if this new paradigm for love was not what a lot of people wanted to hear. Many do not want to think of love as your own creation. It is not what you were taught or how you originally processed the information so you do not want to believe it.

*"The trouble with the world is not that people know too little. But that they know so many things that just aren't so."*
- Mark Twain, American writer 1835-1910

We normally do not like to accept knowledge that is contrary to what we already believe. Instead we like to add more information to what we already believe. One analogy is that your memory grows like a framework or tree. It is a lot easier to add a memory to an existing framework than to remember it all alone. If you want to believe the oak tree story, you grow it by adding oak leaves, not maple leaves.

An example is, if I said to you that James Henderson is a thief, and then I asked you to remember his name, you would find it hard because you don't have a framework (tree) of information on him to add it to.

*"It's hard to teach an old dog new tricks."*

*The pups borrow Stan's phone to show the old dog the local dog park locations.*

You probably would remember he is a thief because you have a some framework in your head on thieves already. Now if I said your uncle was a thief, you definitely could remember that. Because you already have a framework of information on your uncle to add thief to.

The bottom line to this chapter is, I understand if it is hard for some to accept my theory on love. It is a lot easier to add something to and defend your old framework than to create a new one. It is what we all do. By the way, what was the name of that thief again?

*"A scientific truth does not triumph by convincing its opponents and making them see the light, but rather its opponents eventually die and a new generation grows up that is familiar with it."*
- Maxwell Plank, German physicist (1858-1947) when asked about the great scientific discoveries he made during his life.

# QUESTIONS

If my theory that love is your own expectations is to be proven accurate it should hold up under all conditions. A theory should prove itself reliable through repeated testing and confirmation. Although this book is not written for psychologists in the style of a research paper with statistics to back up its claim, I do believe I have made a case for my theory by using everyday examples the average person can comprehend and test for himself/herself.

Here I test my theory under a number of circumstances. I did it by having a variety of people read the book and then ask any personal questions, questions about love or questions they feel the book did not cover. Here are those questions. I hope in this book I have given you a new framework of knowledge so you can answer for yourself those questions you feel the book does not cover.

How and why do we love strangers?

Depending on your upbringing, you will have different levels of expectations for strangers and therefore different levels of love you might project on them. If you grew up in a town and family where you could trust most everybody, you likely will have a first instinct to trust most people. The more people who you trust enough to be around, the more people you have to potentially get close to and have loving relationships with.

If you grew up in a town/family where people would take advantage of you if you trusted them, then your instinct would be to not trust them, making you now more cautious around those you do not know and less likely to meet new people and form new relationships.

But treating someone you know like a stranger could be a positive attitude change, depending on how you treat them now. Sometimes the familiarity or power you have in your relationships lets you treat those close to you worse than you do strangers. Think about it. If you do not treat your spouse, parent, co-worker, sibling, child or friend as well as you do a stranger, you can blame yourself for some of the problems in your relationship. When in doubt, treat everyone with the same respect as you would a powerful boss or beloved grandmother.

*"You catch more flies with honey than you do with vinegar."*
- English proverb

Isn't it somewhat of a cop out to say everyone is different?

Everyone, every circumstance and every relationship is different from the next. Some people love their spouse. Some people love their kids. Some people love their garden. I cannot write about every possible scenario, but what I can do is provide you a theory that covers them all. I feel I have done that. And in spousal love, it does not matter if you are male or female, old or young, gay, straight or confused, this theory covers you all.

Can I love someone I have never met?

Sure. There are many circumstances where a parent and child can grow up without knowing each other. Dads can father children then leave. Moms can put their children up for adoption. But these parents and children know there is someone out there to whom they are related and can imagine who those missing people are. Their illusions for the missing relative could be good or bad, based on facts (pictures and stories told to them) or fiction (pictures and stories told to them). Depending on what you want to do with this lack of information, you could long for the love of this missing relative, hate them for not being there for you, or you could care less. Whatever you can imagine.

Recently my sister and her son (age 45) visited his grandmother, the mother of the father he had never met. The grandmother had never met her grandson before, but she confessed that she had always thought of him and longed to meet him. They arranged a meeting and despite the fact the grandmother and her family had never met my sister and her son before, they presented themselves as loving relatives.

The current television show *Catfish* also illustrates how people fall in love with those they have never met. People online often are not what they claim to be. They might show a fake picture or take on a fake personality in order to impress. But that does not stop people from their imagination and from falling in love. And since there is no personal contact to give the relationship reality, it lets your expectations for them have no bounds.

How do you explain the tingly feeling I got when I met my wife?

Your feelings or emotions are always a personal experience that are hard to explain, label or measure. Your tingly feelings for your new wife were likely labeled by you as love to explain the happiness you felt for winning a mate, securing a sex partner, reducing your loneliness, gaining societal acceptance and imagining your future. But the question I have is: You say you had these feelings when you first met your wife. Why not now? Do you love your wife now? If so, why don't you have those tingly feelings now? And what about the tingly feelings you had for those other women who did not end up being your wife?

The way you can have a different kind of love for your wife now is because you have different expectations for her. In the beginning of your relationship, you were probably apart more, missing each other more and had more unre-alistic expectations than now. Now you live with her and things have changed. Your expectations are different and more realistic now. So your love is different.

Stan: *"The heart doctor said I should watch my diet, exercise and the French sometimes drink a little red wine. This is the only one that's any fun."*

Can I love more than one person?

Of course you can. You can love anything you can imagine. You can love your parent, child, football team, friend, garden and three spouses all at one time if you can handle it. Why not? Most societies say you should not marry more than one person so that rules out legally and morally having multiple husbands or wives, but that does not stop all the fooling around that is not legal or moral. If you cheat on your spouse, does that mean you do not love your him/her? Of course not. You could love them both. You also could come home and find your clothes are on the lawn.

*"I've been in love with the same woman for 41 years. If my wife finds out she'll kill me."*
- Henny Youngman, American comedian 1906-1998

Why would a man leave a devoted wife and mother?

This was a question from a teenage girl whose dad left her mother and the family.

If the man leaves his wife, it is because she is not fulfilling the expectations he has for her. If he was not living up to her expectations, she would be leaving him. It could be this was her fault or his. She might not be fulfilling his realistic needs to be his partner, lover or mother in the relationship. Or more likely, he had unrealistic expectations that she did not fulfill.

Both spouses bring in to a marriage expectations for what the marriage will bring them, whether they are realistic or unrealistic. If your partner or the situation do not meet these expectations, you can feel like your life is not being lived as it should be. Like something is being taken away from you. And you leave to try to find out what you have been missing.

The other day on the radio, I heard a man describe his marriage as one where he works all day, and when he gets home, it's his wife's duty to provide sex to him. He felt that every marriage was this way. This is his expectation for marriage, whether it is realistic or unrealistic. If this is also the wife's expectation for herself, this marriage can continue on to the next challenge. If sex on demand is not what she signed up for, then he will be unfulfilled and she will feel pressured until the couple change or move on.

What is mature love?

I feel mature love is a very important subject because it is most people's ideal for what love is. When we think of the perfect spousal love we aspire for, it is of an old couple holding hands, still happy, and married for a long time. We imagine the couple loved each other at first sight and have had a loving sexual relationship ever since. And maybe some did. Good for them. But it is more likely the couple was brought together by sex, loneliness, arranged marriage, or pregnancy than love at first sight. And it is more likely the couple have had ups and downs, fights and make ups, than a relationship of continuous bliss.

Many love theories teach that love starts out as romantic or passionate and grows into mature or compassionate love. But I feel the success of a relationship is up to the individuals in the relationship becoming mature, not the love. For long-term success, it is more important the couple want to be in the relationship with each other and want to make it work than to be in love. After all, what is more important for you to continue a relationship, being happy or being in love? Are you happy if you have a spouse who cheats on you? No. Are you happy if your spouse gambles away or spends all your money? No. Are you happy if your spouse hits you? No. These are all potential deal breakers. You might love this person for the rest of your life but still know you are better off without him/her.

On the other hand, we all know of marriages that have had difficulties such as violence, infidelity, or money problems, and yet these couples stay together. Many things can contribute to a person staying in a relationship despite the difficulties, such as kids, sex, money, loneliness, love, social standing, comfort, or whatever you personally value. Each of these difficulties and reasons to stay have a different value to each person. For one person infidelity is a relationship breaker, but for another person it is not. For one person staying together for the kids is a priority, for another it is not.

Statistics say that money problems are the number one reason for divorce in the USA. This illustrates how you have expectations for a certain lifestyle in your marriage. If the lifestyle you expected is not met, you might feel unfulfilled and leave. How you weigh the pros and cons of a relationship, to determine whether you will stay or leave, is up to you and how much you want to be in that relationship.

More important to a couple's success is his/her ability to make their marriage work no matter what happens. Some successful marriages start off as arranged by their parents so we know this couple cannot be in love at the start because they do not even know each other. Many people in long lasting relationships do not have sex anymore or might describe themselves as not being in love. Or maybe only one spouse is in love. But that does not mean the relationship will stop. If those in the relationship make the effort and want the relationship to continue, it will, despite the difficulties.

When you have a long lasting relationship with a spouse or friend, many of the expectations you have for them are not expectations anymore, because they have already been realized. This person has already been there with you for years, through thick and thin. They have already helped you raise your kids, grand kids and they are with you helping you in your senior years now. And you still have it going for you that you want to be there for each other. If a long married couple's love is different than that of a young couple's love, it is because the long married couple have a history with each other. They have realistic maps of each other with realistic expectations.

Stan. *"I knew for our love to mature we needed to have personal growth. I was just hoping it would be yours."*

Doesn't everybody know this already? The simple idea that love is your own thoughts or expectations.

No, they do not, no one teaches us this. Most people do not even try to think about what love is, much less conjure up their own theory for it. And despite the fact that this could be as obvious as the nose on your face to someone, I still cannot find anybody that has ever said love is self created before, anywhere.

Is love worth the effort?

This book cannot possibly tell you what is worth your effort and what is not, or who is worth your effort and who is not. This book cannot tell you if love will make you happy or sad. You have your own individual expectations for what love and a spousal relationship means to you, and you use these expectations to guide you. If you feel a person is worth your effort to try and create a loving relationship with them, then that is your decision. If they are not worth your effort, then that is also your decision. The same could be said for any type relationship you wish to start. This book, at best, suggests a theory to tell you what is going on in your head when you feel like you are in love. Hopefully you can use this knowledge to help you make the best decisions possible for you. To answer, is love worth the effort? The best answer I can give is that it is up to you.

What should I do if I am getting married or choosing a spouse?

I think most of us know the answer to this question, it is just not what we normally do. You should take your time and get to know your future spouse as best you can before you marry them. You should have long discussions about your future. You should ask every question you can think of and listen to every question your spouse can think of. You should spend lots of time with them. Hopefully, this will reveal both of your expectations for marriage to reduce the number of surprises in your future. If you are in the Catholic church they would want for you and your spouse to have their counseling before marriage. If you are Catholic, this sounds like a good idea.

Unfortunately, that is not what many of us do. Many of us let sex guide our relationship. You figure if you are having sex with someone, this must be love. You will figure out the rest later. After all, in a monogamous relationship, sex is only supposed to be with your spouse. You can have friendship, live together, have intimate conversations, love each other, grow old with each other or go places with each other but you are only supposed to be having sex with your spouse.

*"Don't have sex, man. It leads to kissing and pretty soon you have to start talking to them."*
- Steve Martin, American comedian

So many of us end up married to our sex partner instead of our friend, especially if you and your sex partner created a child. And then if the sex cannot keep the relationship together, you can end up with someone you do not know or do not like. Our divorce rates prove this. The correct answer to having a long term relationship is easy. Just find someone you want to be with forever, and who wants to be with you forever.

How does love end?

If love is having positive expectations for someone, then the end of love is when you stop having positive expectations for them. You could stop having expectations immediately or over time, but love does not end when a person leaves you or if they die. That is because your thoughts do not stop when they leave you or if they die.

If your spouse is unfaithful to you or is violent with you, it could end your love of them right now. If you cannot imagine being in love with a person who is unfaithful or is violent then that says it all, you cannot imagine it. Your expectations for your relationship never included your spouse hitting you or your spouse being with another lover. So if his/her actions have caused you to stop having positive expectations for them, and now you only see the negative side of them, this can be your love ending.

Your love could also slowly disappear if the expectations you had for you or your spouse slowly disappear. If over time your spouse is letting you know that they are not trying, they are not your friend or they do not care about you, it can wear you down and take away any positive expectations you have for your spouse. Or, over time if you are letting your spouse know that you are not trying, you are not their friend, you do not care about them, this is certainly wearing them down and taking away positive expectations they might feel towards you. This can be love slowly disappearing.

Over time you and your spouse (or friend) could drift apart if you are keeping score, and one of you is behind on the score. We often have expectations for our friends and spouses that we put equal efforts into a relationship. Efforts could include money, time, sex or whatever one feels is currency in the relationship. If one person feels he/she is putting out more effort than his/her spouse (or friend), over time this can build up to be a problem. This is not something we normally talk about because it makes us look selfish, but we all know what the score is so we know if we are being taken advantage of. You can say you do not do this, but you know you do. Even if you are a giver, you only give for so long when someone is taking advantage of you.

Sibling love.

Of all the circumstances that a single theory for love has to cover, sibling love seems to encompass them all. You have such high expectations for your siblings. They should be just like you. They should be loved equally by the parents. They should think and do anything you would do. If you do something for them, then they should want to do something for you. You are not talking strangers here. You are in the same family, the same name, living in the same house, sleeping in the same room. You are expected to stick together, defend each other, and love each other.

Those are a lot of expectations to live up to. And if you expect something and you do not get it, you can get angry. Angry at a person you cannot get away from. A person where you might have to sleep in the same room, share things, ride in the back seat together, do chores together, vacation together, get punished together, wear each other's clothes and so on. Parents often demand child siblings do things with each other that we would not expect adults to be able to do with each other. It is no wonder why siblings seem to fight or hate each other just as often as they love each other.

Back when my daughter and son were young, I was watching them play a computer game with my daughter's friend. My daughter's friend was sitting in one chair, and my son and daughter were sharing the second chair. If you asked my daughter who she liked more at that moment, her friend or her younger brother, she would have chosen her friend. And yet she was sharing a seat with her brother. The expectations on her brother to share the chair were greater than that of her friend despite the fact she wanted to be with her friend more.

If your sibling lives up to your expectations for his/her, you can be very close. Closer than anybody. After all, you slept in the same room, shared experiences, wore each other's clothes and shared the same house. But if you have an event in your past where your sibling does not live up to your expectations, it is equal to your mom leaving you on the side of the road without jumper cables. You expected to be able to count on your sibling's support, but you cannot. That is why when you sit down to your next family gathering, you could still be remembering how your siblings did you wrong many years before.

I grew up the youngest of seven kids. My oldest sister was twenty-years-old, married and out of the house by the time I was born. We have never lived in the same town at the same time. While my other siblings and I had the typical drama that siblings have, I had few interactions with my oldest sister. And while the middle siblings had plenty of stories to tell about her over the years, none of it had happened to me. I had no expectations for her, good or bad. So even though she is my sister, I had few feelings for her, good or bad. Since I do not have the prejudices for my oldest sister built up in me like the middle siblings, I can have a relationship with her without emotional baggage.

Do I need intimacy to have love?

Intimacy is a unique word in that it is defined as two people having sex or as having a close friendship or secret.

But it could also mean the two people are having sex and a friendship at the same time. We normally assume if you are having sex and are friends, then you are in love, but you do not have to be. You can have sex without love or you can have love without sex. Furthermore, you can have an intimate conversation or relationship with someone without sex or love.

The definition for intimacy, like love, can be different for each person. For some, eye contact or a touch on the shoulder can be an intimate moment, for others it will not. I feel that saying "I love you" can be a form of intimacy since the purpose is to link people together. The words let two people know their relationship is different than a typical one. It is up to you to define what intimacy is to you and for you to decide how important intimacy is in your relationships.

Why didn't my parents tell me they loved me? Why did my friend's family do it and not mine?

Maybe you should have asked your parents. Maybe they thought they did tell you, or show you in other ways. It is possible your parents were never told they were loved as a child, so they did not feel they needed to tell you. What if your parents wanted you to tell them, "I love you," more often? I still say you should ask them.

Every family is different. Every individual is different. Every generation is different. Often times the next generation or the next sibling do the opposite of what is occurring because they do not like what is happening to them. If one set of parents did not profess their love for their children, the kids might make sure they tell the grand kids they love them. If one parent is strict, then the other parent might be lenient. If the first child is messy, the second child might be extra clean to make up for it. The point is, who you are is affected by your family tree, your parents above you, your siblings beside you and your kids below you. And in this case you were affected by your friend's family, who told their kids they loved them. It could be you would not have noticed the difference if not for your friend's family (It's all their fault). If you are a parent now, it is up to you to move on from this baggage and do what you think is right for the next generation. It is up to you to answer your kid's questions.

*"The long and the short define each other. High and low depend on each other. Before and after follow each other."*
- Lao Tzu, Chinese philosopher, 604BC-531BC Tao Te Ching, 2

# CLOSING

In closing, I will give some recommendations based on the contents of this book. The first is something I gained in writing this book. I now feel it is easier to say *I love you* than I did before. I feel free to spread some good vibrations with it, I do not anticipate any repercussions from it, so why not.

Another recommendation I can give is, work hard to create a realistic map of the world so you can have realistic expectations for it. The less misinformation you have in your map (the fewest lies you tell yourself), the less the map will take you down the wrong path. A realistic map will give you truthful information and allow you to make better decisions based on facts.

Since a main topic in this book is expectations, let's go there. One way to deal with expectations is to set the bar low, don't sweat the small stuff, or have no expectations at all. This can mean you have fewer frustrations, but it will not solve everything. If you are trying to achieve a goal of winning a mate, getting straight A's, earning enough money for your home, selling so many units or winning a game, you do not want realistic or low expectations, you want high expectations. So the important thing to learn here is that in any situation you should know what you are expecting of yourself and know what others are expecting of you. And if possible, correct the expectations if they are inappropriate.

In this book I proposed that if you love someone you have expectations of him/her. So, if someone loves you, they are having expectations of you. It is common for a spouse (or others) to have expectations of you, but sometimes they do not tell you what they are. They might not want you to know, or they might not even know themselves. It is difficult to live up to someone's expectations if you do not know what they are. Lack of communication about expectations is a common problem in any type of relationship. So do your best to know what you expect of others and what others expect of you.

You also need to have realistic expectations of love. Love is not a force that holds us together or when cupid shoots us with an arrow. Our love for someone (or something) is what we create in our own head. One should not expect love to grow towards us or be waiting for us. If you are experiencing love, it has come from you. If your spouse is in love with you it is what they create in their own head. A child or parent's love for each other is what they create in their own heads. This is not what the romance novel teaches us. But if you want a realistic map of love, then this is the reality.

*"We are not born with maps: we have to make them, and the making requires effort. The more effort we make to appreciate and perceive reality, the larger and more accurate our map will be. But many do not want to make this effort."*
- M Scott Peck, psychologist (1936-2005) - The Road Less

Traveled: A new psychology of love, traditional values and
spiritual growth, 1978

Love, or any relationship, is what you make it. If you
are to experience love, you need to take a chance and have
expectations of someone. And if someone is to to love you,
they need to take a chance and have expectations of you. If
you try to make your relationship good, and your spouse (or
friend) tries to make it good, most times it will work. Not
every time. But that is no reason not to take a chance. Take
a chance.

*"The end of the world is coming. So I'd have a good time if
I were you."*
- Neil Rogers, American talk radio host (1942-2010)

**END**

www.ingramcontent.com/pod-product-compliance
Lightning Source LLC
Chambersburg PA
CBHW031328040426
42443CB00005B/253